The Perfect Unravelling of the Spirit

The Perfect Unravelling of the Spirit

Irene Marques

We acknowledge the support of the Canada Council for the Arts for our publishing program. We also acknowledge support from the Government of Ontario through the Ontario Arts Council.

We acknowledge the financial support of the Government of Canada through the Canada Book Fund for our publishing activities

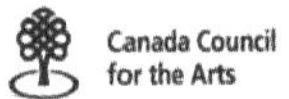

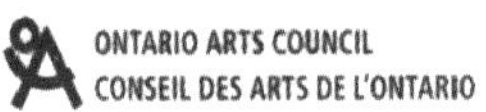

Canadä

Cover design by Peggy Stockdale

Library and Archives Canada Cataloguing in Publication

Marques, Irene,
The perfect unravelling of the spirit : poems / Irene Marques.

ISBN 978-1-894770-96-5

I. Title.

PS8626.A683P47 2012 C811'.6 C2012-905394-5

Printed and bound in Canada by Coach House Printing

TSAR Publications
P. O. Box 6996, Station A
Toronto, Ontario M5W 1X7
Canada
www.tsarbooks.com

To my father
To my mother
To Isabel

Contents

Mayando in Adsamo

In the eyes of the neighbours she was a saint
who did not fear earthy ways
or slow down during the rains
she would travel long distances
only to meet floral incantations
and bring them to the starving

In the eyes of the people
she possessed the ways of the world
and the collars of the winters
the trees of the Himalayas
the carnations of Singapore
the lilies of Senegal
the cedars of Andaluzia
the jasmine of Mongolia

In the eyes of the peasants
she came back every year
to adorn their lonely souls
and bring the adoring smells of fresh life

Every year
Mayando in Adsamo

Washed My Sheets Last Night

I washed my sheets last night, slept like an angel, imagined
a childhood and goats and open fields and Isabel dancing
abracadabra with me

Washed my sheets last night and my body rolled into an oblivion
where all is ephemeral and you live in pleasant shadowy caves,
walk your soul to the stars, twinkling wisdom smiling, telling you
stories of your dead father and all the other relatives,
the congregation of the hereafter all there, their soul became yours,
you are all there was and all there will ever be

I washed my sheets last night with floral scents and eucalyptus
oils to breathe purely and dream and wake up strong and clear,
body and soul ready to endure another day of wars and hunger
turning lives into dust while we sit watching, and buying bottles
of Acqua Cologne

Washed my sheets last night so I could visit the frogs
and hear the chants of Gregorian monks, incantations to the abode
of intemporal dwelling, where blue is the colour of peace
and solace for tired limbs

Washed my sheets last night just to be with Isabel

Dreaming of Peaches

I dream of peaches all day long
when I am in the ideal stage of eternal life

I cuddle inside the invisible air when I enter the river of nothingness
enchanted by mystical monks who sing to me from inside the
darkness of their capes
as though eager to hide what they have discovered after years of
solitude

I settle scores with the mute corners of the world when I sit down
and communicate with the living wise mistress, finally not afraid
of being alone

I awake in the morning feeling I have run the countryside of my
youth
I have waved my body slowly in the green grasslands, waiting for
the eureka moment to take me to the solstice of life
that the goats visited in the mountains of my youth, bells
proclaiming sanctity and the yearning of blood, eager to continue
the long line of life

And then I cry, in utter concentration, with the expectation
that newness may visit me

I cannot stop dancing now—in this morning of hollowness
and incantation

Matted Paper

I am made out of matted paper
colourful silk perfecting me from head to toe, limb to limb
I cast shadows over the short inklings
to make them grand and long and long lasting

I extend my hands to the lines beneath the train stations of the world
I cut across grass fields and recover the white hands of Isabel
when she in the last memory of her soul in this world came to me

She came and then left the dark church where repressed priests
and old ladies called her *noiva em branco para Deus,*
because even God needs a virgin to feast upon

I touch her thick black hair still hanging to the lust of life
I dance with its waves, like her soul leaving the dark place
to enter the open fields and valleys of our childhood
when we guarded the sacred goats of God
and screamed to the world and its blindness

I am made out of flying kits and matted paper and this way reach
between here and there, extending endlessly to meet Isabel
by the river shore, by the valley green, by the high mountain
where goats play together like sibilas of divine madrigals
sung by nothing and heard by everything

I am made of paper
matted colours that scream life and love and soul
I am made of wind and grass, passing trains
and tumultuous oceanic waves
I am big and large

I can walk between here and all that there is
give me your hand, come and laugh with me

Emerging

I have emerged from the dark winter and suddenly all I want is
light, light
my body discovers itself under your savvy hands and the moist
of your mouth and all I see is water, water and me and you swimming,
like a course to the transcendent and a rose of the untold

My mother's words fade and the priest's sermons leave
my tightly crossed legs and I open myself to you, I open myself
to the flight we are capable of apprehending

I get up in the morning and all I see is sun, all I want is
to wear dresses, purple and white, with yellows and roses,
like a spring that you, only you could give birth to

I am a child again, naked as I was when my mother opened
herself to give me a chance in this world, when she opened
herself after so many years of hard labour having already given birth
to countless boys and girls, babies crying for love

I go out and I dance in the garden of the fall about to begin,
I dream of the spring and the summer to come, how I will
glide through the earth in flowing dresses and round open skirts
just to show you how much I love myself and my body,
that body tamed by sermons of iron preached for centuries
by perverse priests and a hungry mother whose body has reached
the limits of selfness to eject life into this world

I float above myself, I dwell in you, you in me, so that what we are
is a dream come true, a story that I have spent my entire life writing,
filling in the gaps, in thousands of white pages in which I wrote
novels that still had not happened

I go out and I melt under you, under the sun, the God that gave
me me and dreamed you
I say slowly under my breath, "This is what I have been looking
for"
I say, "Please love me and take me and make my fully dreamed
dream come true so that I have a feast and a beautiful poem,
or a novel, to write to the world and tell to it
how the sublime has not yet abandoned this earth that cries
where bloody murderers walk freely committing prophecies of the
untold"

Please love me like that, like the dream that I dreamed
and then spent nights crying over, during those long dark winters
hiding my body in the dark shades of black holes, like a princess
afraid of being raped by men who do not know how to walk the earth
without committing sacrilege and stepping on the rightfully beautiful

Body in the Dark

Marvellous sounds emitting light from the bottom of my being

Down there where my lover has not yet gone, blind with my
surface beauty and the soothing moment it gives him, ephemeral
lullaby for an immature child who cannot yet handle the greatness
of love, which brings trips to the mountains and rides to the third
ring of the earth, where uranium meets carbon,
where fire dances on water and sings to the wind

Sometimes when I feel lonely I guide him to my bottom,
to that place where I know I live the most,
the sturdy floor where I want him to meet me
so we can truly dance the movement
I know we can master

And sometimes, when he is lonely and his chest can no longer
endure the profound state of human bareness, he allows me
to take him there, at least to the beginning of my marvellous
window where the light of me shines more than Circinus, blinding
him to nonexistence, it is there that we both embrace the self
that is greater than us and find solace from the street vendors of
Kaduna, men and women wearing large bright flowing clothes,
offering fruits to those who walk with bare feet on the running
and uncertain deserts of Northern Nigeria like angels from the
underground

Body in the dark is when I chew myself slowly and add your saliva
to my own; it is when we both kiss our own selves through one
another's mouth, like strangers returning our bodies to ourselves
through the live flooding river that runs in our veins

Body in the dark, mine and yours, the black forest of immemorial
remembrances

pink shadows and swallows flying through the veins of the universe
so that we all become joined at the navel, cataclysms of nothing

My body and yours
in the dark

Water and Breathing

In the middle of time when the day has stopped and I am tired of
waiting
and numb from things that go on repeating
then I dance outside of myself, and I do the following exercises:

First I chant a line to my node, the one under the scale of the
narrow
ladder that I would climb when I was a child, taking unplanned
rides through the metaphor of time
and the fields of my grandfather

Then I raise my head to the sky and search for the spots between
the moon and the sun, the lines where the many other stars
and planets might live, where many beings, humans and others,
have chosen to spend the slow line of the unmoved unmoving
days, floating in awe in that rich density that is black matter

After that I dance alone in the middle of the night, so much and
at such high speed that I become one with the firmament, my
body reaching the extension and incandescence of the stars,
I pulsating with light in the centre of gravity and with the weight
of time upon my being

And now I fully feel time and the happenings of history
I am entire, not alone, but exhausted from the pains of the many
and from the weight of all the matter that has made me and you,
and all the stars and planets

Breathing water and air and fire
I am the Nile
infinite water bathing itself and all the rest

Travelling in the Shadow Light

I am going to the moon
tomorrow, when I wake up, I'll be sinking in the gulf of air above
scratching solitude away with my cottony nails and my languid
limbs

In the light of the nether, you and I will join the navel
of remarkable lines
lines and lines of being before it became a speaking agent in the
deathly common language adored by the slaves of today

Markers of marked, transformed, transferred souls
that have long left this side of being
to enter the other zone

Characters who have nothing to fear, for they live in androgynous
matted spheres where to dance is to love, where to hug is to sing
in voice and body, and in different languages, entangled tongues,
endlessly
and purposefully mumbling about true meaning so that the world
makes sense and we can really mate with one another

Finally sanctified saints who have arrived at the cathedral
they were meant to inhabit

Loving the World

Loving the world as it is, is the most profound encounter with the self
from morning to dawn you stare at the sky and every body
dwelling in that unending abode appears like magic delivered to you
by a kind god well aware of the days that are hard to take in
thankfully

Like the day when Gaddafi told his people that freedom was what
he called it or when you broke your inner wing for the very first
time because the love that you loved and spent years cultivating
in your inner being did not come to be

Loving the world as it is, is hard sometimes and the only way
to make bearable the ticking of the iron clock is to swallow in air
from the top of the mountains, that sacred peak we ascend when
darkness falls upon the tiles of our home because we forgot that
we ourselves are gods and have in us the beautiful light that can
bring benevolent solar storms to this sacred ground upon which
our soles tread

Loving the world as it is, is the most profound promise you can
make to yourself and the only way to make it better
by accepting that you are the captain of this astounding ship
this glorious ball that floats in the immense universe, suspended
simply by the will of gravity and the mathematics of planetary
equilibrium

This simple perfect universe, where stars become planets
only to allow life to grow and grass to spring up so that peaceful
cows and elegant gazelles, rabbits and crickets, can run and sing
and do summersaults in the air

Composing the symphony of my soul and the limbs of your body

Ariana at the Window

Spilling away her eyes,
this woman mourns what she can't have
and forgets to adore what walks under her feet
so very close to the centre of her soul

With dark eyelashes,
longer than the wings of angels,
she forgets how to kiss the borders of her own body
and embrace the dancing glittering dust all around her
miraculous snowflakes that refresh your membrane with
a hint of peppermint
and a breeze of May flowers

Her arms spread,
and eyes longing for the astounding infinity beyond her reach
she wears that sadness that leaves no doubt to the wise onlooker
who has learned that God is everywhere you touch and see
everywhere you eat and drink, like a sponge when truly grabbed
giving you all you ever need, the dream of the sublime
and the shades of the morning twilight

Ariana at the window, still young
and sad already despite all her magnificent beauty
one day, one hopes, her beauty will truly reveal itself and those eyes,
eyelashes longer than the wings of an angel
will play at summer summersaults forever
to meet the long rainbows that cross between here
and now, between here and forever

Ariana, Ariana . . .
the world is all there offering you all you need,

the rest is mere illusion of the yet un-awakened Buddha
living in the middle of your chest, breathing strong and sure
beneath those bountiful breasts with nipples like clusters of cherries
awaiting to be eaten by life

Breathing the Opaque Sun

I breathe the water that comes from the bottom of myself,
immersed in the nose of my ears I can hear and smell the sea
and its salt secrets, revealed to me in slow undulating movements—
like magical clean flies transporting the apocalyptic souls of
things that no longer are

I slow down and rest on my knees for long seconds, extending
time to its end, revealing the concluding messages of an angel
that has passed by me leaving behind
in the subcutaneous cells of my deeper members,
the stories of civilizations, rows of people chanting
the collective unconscious of a universe,
that wide, wide murmur that cannot be shut down

I revel in the somnolence of the empathic sphere of quotidian
remembrances and in the noise of all that we have done
and thought about doing

I challenge myself to push the utopia further, like Marx,
like Wollstonecraft, like Gandhi, like Mandela, like Mother Teresa,
like the fruit vendor in Tunisia, trying to feed the dreams
of a hungry population hungry for meat to fatten itself to an
oblivious excess that can only lead to spiritual dementia, people
no longer learning the multiple languages that being possesses,
mute to wisdom, saying no to the eyes of life

I inscribe memories of times to come on the surface of the
opaque sun, screaming for more, screaming for justice
recalling white candles and abundant bread
I slow down and speak to the angels on my knees
Bless me God, bless me please

The House in the Deodar Trunk

In the house where I lived there existed a document
hidden in the old trunk buried underneath my mother's
underground compound

I was small then, but I knew, and I knew ever since I made
entrance into this world, that there was an ark where my mother
kept untold secrets, chess games she did not want anyone
to learn, as though ashamed of her libertine past, or perhaps
just acting as a guardian of important truths, a true goddess of
the ancient body of law, that philosophy of being that does not
want the red messages to be put at risk by leaving them accessible
to the hands of the brutes, those who have not yet learned how to
keep secrets and taste the body of God in that simple white wafer
offered by the priest at Easter, when the days are becoming clear,
light and charcoal, reaching the middle stage, the beautiful one
that is neither there nor here

Before I could walk, and when I was only able to lay there and
stare at the ceiling like a baby, I would see that trunk in detail,
I would stare at it in the eye of my mind and I would see it with
such precision that I could almost smell the cedar wood that made
it so after the Indian tree died to give life to another life, and by so
doing permitted the transformation of bodies and the making of
dreams for humans to dwell in, and even though I could only see
it from the outside I knew there lay inside it profound messages
that would fascinate me ad infinitum, future treats that I would
eternally savour, enigmas that I would spend my entire life
discovering, making me forever an adult-child, perpetually
engaged in a wonder of gradually discovered mysteries, slowly
divining the divine, not willing to mourn disenchantment

I knew then that when I started crawling, the first voyage I would make would be to the place where the trunk was hidden so that I could confirm whether my baby vision was in fact based on a material veridic existence, and so the day my arms and legs knew the strength required had come, my mind took me down to the place where the thing was, and just like I had seen it before there it was, and the deodar smell too, that reminiscence of what it was before it became what it now was, a demonstration of how vigorous old love is and how potent the first wound of life can be

I stared at it awhile and although a part of me knew that I wanted to open it and see what it was guarding inside its belly, the other part of me also knew that that very act would be unwise for it would damage the happiness of my long future ahead, and with that in mind, the mind of my toddler self, I receded into the other parts of my mother's house and in that process I found things of the highest kind and quality, superior objects which gave me the entertainment I needed and the growth into to my upcoming existence

Passing the Passage

Under the tip of my tongue I grasp for words, sounds before
meaning that will say who you are, how you lived and how you
left us to go away and swim in the other current under the node
of dark nymphs, those goddesses that sing of winds
below the sphere and breathe breaths under, under your skin

My mother sighs constantly giving voice to those kisses she never
gave him even in the moments she really wanted to forget
the repression of the Catholic Church and the sombre sermons
of Padre Lévito

I want to cry for you, a real cry from the right side of my soul,
I want to but it does not come, not now, not yet, as though to
avoid the time passed between the moment you were born and
the moment you died, I want to cry but I am not willing, not yet
ready to emerge from the full summers of uncontained hydrangeas,
those wild crazed flowers that do not know what thirst is,
bursting into miscegenated colours never before seen

Under my tongue I compose meanings and words outside of the
alphabet, which do not yet say how I feel about your passage
to the other nether, after this nether full of fulls

I think thoughts of guilt, voices that tell me I could have saved
you, given you more days to live, more walks in the full vines
of your many lands, or that when you died I should have been
there, easing the moment of the last blink of your heart, or should
at least have lifted the veil of the coffin to stare at your body and
touch your cold hands directly, like I did with your face
scaring away the flies impatient to feast upon you and your sacred
nothing

I could have or I should have because nothing is enough
in the face of your timely death

The Days

The days may be gone but the light still simmers through your
bones, I learn how to become mute through the orifices
of your nose and I do not expect any compensation for the
minutes lost in adoration meandering through each part of your
body

I watch the movement of your barely moving hand
and I remember how it is to live fully and then suddenly be assaulted
by the weight of days as if you are in me and me in you

I touch your forehead and perceive through your breathing skin
that your life and mine (in this state) are but ephemeral moments
that go away in less than the blink of a butterfly's wing

I look around your room and concentrate on details that have
missed my eyes before but which now appear as vivid and
fundamental as a fresh morning when your senses lazily awaken
and life makes the most sense: your blood flowing slowly but surely
to meet the challenges of a long day

I smell your body and the approaching decay and I imagine
the beauty of your limbs when you were a child running
unimpeded as beautiful as a morning mercy

I put my head close to yours and hear the inner thoughts your
dying soul is reminiscing about, and I imagine all the dreams
you have had through your long life, from birth to this moment,
dreams of utter beauty and victory in life, from task-filled days
when your body felt the most alive and able, the most noble,
to days when mornings and nights gave you moments that
nothing can recreate, moments of simple merciful beauty like the
gradual darkening of the approaching dusk or the arrival
of a new awakening clarity with all its promises,
after the night has passed
and the dreams have left its vivid notes

Your days are all there, entangled in your wrinkled body
which I observe with the saddness of a daughter
losing her father, imagining the loss of her own body,
a body still young and yet already feeling in its universal memory
that its days too are counted

For we are nothing but intersecting light
passing through or the momentary beauty of the horse
cavalcading through the open fields

Mimesis

Marbles in your hands, and you and I mumbling about memories
that only time will tell. I came to the world more than ten
thousand years ago when Saturn was not yet visible to the eye and
Apolinia emitted only scarce slight sounds as though speaking
to the blind with acute listening.

I woke up one day and my round naked legs told me that love
could be found in infinite ways, the only requirement being that
I extend my body fully on the grass and inhale the sun's energy,
that great feeling-matter that possesses memories
of the beginning of the world, before the Nile became a river
and the great Isis took over the destiny of the country,
fiercely domesticating unruly men, like a savage priestess
marching to a land that she knew was rightfully hers.

Only a moment ago I dreamed of caramel shadows under my
skin breathing instants of love and messages of the reign
of the god Ciprius,
the faraway solemn Magus sending me letters of beautiful posts
found at the bottom of nothing, when suddenly everything makes
sense and madrigal songs become rosaries of purple and yellow
shadows, marvelous scentful endless, meandering in me like
Gregorian chants extending the spirit to unnameable places,
corners of decades and decades of aloneness suddenly becoming
open windows, visionary true stars announcing the untold beautiful.

I say: "Only now do I see the marble of my hand playing with the
fingertips of your inner molecular energy. Only now do I wipe
my tears in your face, tears not of sadness but of beautiful days,
days I have suddenly discovered after centuries of loss
and dazed dark infinity, walking in the sombre soles of utter
annulment.

I know now, today, in this moment. I know why I was born
why I wanted to cross the long wide ocean to the other side,
entering the new world, that wide plaza full of greens and
incendiary landscapes, leaving me exhausted when fall arrives
and winter blazes, blinded with the astonished beauty of a bride
finally married.

I scan the morning to see how the horizon carries the dawn
and in the midst of this awakening matinal experience, when my
body
is still warm and meek with the remembrance of yours in me,
I remember the other side, when my mother and I would
get up early to travel down south, two women at different stages
of their lives joined by need and filial love.

I may die today but if I do there will be nothing to regret
because I will have met you at the crossroads of existence,
that moment of sudden light and meaning when everything
and everyone meets and the world no longer feels like a desolate
place crying under the weight of the misery of unfulfilled human
desires.

I may die today but it will not matter because life will have
visited me fully and my body and soul will fly happy,
soothed by the moment, gliding to the other side of the river so that
at last and in awe I will be the found Queen
finally arriving at her sacred mortuary.

Mimesis is my name

Metamorphosis of the Soul

Just last night I was immersed in the old lonely nights of times
past dreaming of pure love and crying out of utter pain for you
and me, the couple that never happened

Just last night I moved my body in my single and narrow bed,
the bed of a woman who has waited for the sun to arrive and
enter each moment of her roughed body, where marks of unclean
hands keep appearing even after the intrusive lovers have long left,
as if I, a being chained to the nodes of the past, suffer
the trauma of colonialism like the many black men and women
who still carry its mark in the shining of their darkened hollow eyes

Just last night I stayed up all night writing a letter to an unknown
man whose soul I keep dreaming in my moments of unclouded
judgment

And just last Saturday, before the feast of the sacred Sabbath
when I took a deep bath in the River Melnon to cleanse my hurt
body,
I leaned towards the floor with my hand praying to the land down
south, summoning the angels and the ancient Shaman
of the other beautiful continent

And just last Sunday, I got up before sunrise, defying the laziness
of my body to go out to the veranda and stare at the darkened
scarlet horizon, that place where after some careful concentration
I could see the possibility of you and me, a couple that could be

I stayed there for a long while looking at all the colours of the
morning and discerning which ones would carry the message
of your secrets, and after that long while that took me outside
of myself, making me lose the single diamond I carry under my

scratched skin, after that long while, I came again to myself
fully revived and certain of your arrival, sooner or later

A letter by post
A whistle of the happy man
A voice

Just last night . . .

Your Ink Is My Ink

My body is full of ink
imprinted by you, through the lines of your bone marrow
that you slipped through me in moments of utter concentration
when you descended from the heavens that usually occupy your
mind and wither your body, when you descended from there and
stayed with me day and night without interruption, like a blanket
of warmth that covers me from head to toe, filling me
with graceful murmurs of sermons incanted by the enlightened
Dalai Lama that lives within you, that saint whose throne has
been robbed by degenerate politicians, who see nothing more
than the cold chains of production and refuse to find solace in the
mysteries of the unseen and in the silent nights of dark winters

I felt you then fully, allowing yourself to be deferred into me
so that my loneliness and yours could stop hurting for a moment,
making the world our full house, the place where nothing
is missing and the only thing we need is us,
together in a moment of sudden and complete encounter, after
an eternity of waiting alone by the desolate window of a seemingly
empty world where not a full breathing being could be detected

My body is full of ink, your colour mixing with mine forming
waves of worldly surprises and translucent rainbows
spreading from here to the faraway, from now to tomorrow,
like lost marvels of tropical Caribbean pearls that shone before
Columbus arrived and killed the enchanted Arawak

I pass my hands through my body and I see you in the open
humid pores of my skin, imagining days past and days to come,
missing you more and more, wishing I could finally
completely have you
I lie down in bed and listen carefully for the planes above

attempting to land, bringing you to me and me to you
so we can make babies and adore one another eternally

I do that, for the only way life and love can happen is if we allow
each to be and sit silently between us, on a long winter night
or a deadly boring afternoon of a summer Sunday, when
everything stops and nothing matters except the utter nakedness
of being and the ability to find solace, against the odds of
existentialist nausea, that dark empty oppresive cloud of Sartre
and Camus

I love you like this and like that and I paint your ink upon mine
constantly, calling you to me and me to you so that our future
radiant child can finally be born and I can dance in the midst of
the plasma wound that comes out of a fertile woman
after she has loved fully and ejected that love into the world,
making the cold streets of our maze more bearable
and easy to the touch of our hurt feet

My ink is your ink
your ink is my ink
this is the bleeding that I prefer, washing myself in its blurred
colours when red, black, and white, and all that is between, merge
to give birth to a dancing star
My ink is your ink

Come, or call me, when you can
before I die again, like I did many times before coming across you
in that unseemingly unexpected way
that road that I forced myself to enter after centuries of utter
isolation
and fear of the hurt that men can bring to women
and the other way too

The Currents

I would not know how to spell your name or mine
with the letters in the alphabet

I would not know how to jump rationally to the impossibilities
of catastrophic seasons with burning sand and magnetic rains

I would not know, but I would know how to open your body
in slow mediated steps and anoint it with mercury from the stars
and dreams from the moistened tears of the moon

I would know how to do that so you obtain the cure you deserve
and I expel the songs of unheard solemnity and unadulterated
faiths brought slowly from the depth of my rivers
and the uncanniness of my soul

My song is yours and yours mine
If you allow for the possibility to become visible
in the twinkle of an eye

Avoiding Time

I avoid days and nights felt with the deep knife of time,
that clock that cuts through each cell of your tall body
and you no longer know what living really means

I run from the days and the nights like a knight on a black horse
with no reigns, oblivious to the dangers of the carved mountain
peaks and the depths of the rivers and the wakes of great waves

I ride firmly, acceding to the horse's thirst just enough to live
and when I reach the end of a bad day I exhale with sublime
elation for at last I have evaded the weighty sorrow
of the hours that burn you deep and stop your life

I am better now, I have reached the light of time, that zone
when being no longer feels weighed by the centuries gone before
and the people who have felt sorrow before

I am better now

The Silence of the Rains

In my silent dreamless nights I name things without names
I pour my blood and the juice of my porous cells onto the ink
of the long canvas of the world and I stay there for eternity
staring at the beauty that the nameless mute can produce

I dance in oblivion moving to the freedom of the canvas
and the music of the people of the world

Each person is free
is herself and himself and itself

There is no incarnation of evil
Clean sheet of my eternal beautiful utopia
The Arcadia of all times

The one I search for every night when my dreams don't come,
and I, hungry for the stunning trans-incendiary, play somersaults
to the palpable invisible that resides at the bottom of myself
in that line where I march, integral, the queen of my self

And I see you too, there in that space, the elemental element
of our intricate collective bodily mass, in that study line
where cleanliness is frozen in the silent dance of the rains,
where the Arcades Project becomes the eloquent
forever-lasting house of being, not camouflaged by the brilliant
curtains
of the époque's fast-moving trains

that strangle my silence and shatter my shadow

The Capacities of Worms

Living below the light they seem unknowing creatures—crawling
beneath the true logic of being that enlightens the wise people of
our world

Slow and slummy, lazy sticks of the nothing populating the dark
mud or the dirty anonymous rivers that wash the underground
maps of rings composing the circle that sustains us all and allows
us to stare at the stars in dark blind nights, like the limbo
of limbos where mayday is the always expected message

Look at the moon and imagine the breathing in, very minute
angles, madness of the senses when the soul incarnates into
a big black horse, the sublime apocalyptic animal of the unending
universe, the day announcing itself in the midst of the darkest
greatest night I inhabit, entering the meditated unmediated space
of yesterday

Like now when I encircle you in circles, like dances or rings
of annual perpetual Talmudic verses or the seasons from Chinese
ancient times, the true character of *The Art of War,* telling you how
to attain power and the limpid elevation of the soul
by being acutely aware of the surrounding terrain and the waters
that crush you into dust and flying air, if you forget the heaviness
of your season and the pain of your body, then you hear the
sublime fatal clock of the unforgetful undying pace of life

Like now when I lose you, finding you again through the spaces
that move in the between-the-lines of the between-of-my-fingers

Like now when the worm that I am breaks into circles of mellow
yellows, infinite trains, or cataracts of seeing
Like now

Too Much Love

There is so much love in the world
and everyone is crying of loneliness

There is so much love in the world
and I sit alone in my lonely invisible angle

I stare at the world and watch its tears roll down my eyes
bathing me with your pain and yours and yours

Why do we do this? Sit alone at an angle when all we want
is the solace of each other's hands and tears washing away our
pain?

Why do we stare at each other's pain when all we need is love and
love and love again?

I sit alone at an invisible angle and I let myself watch the tears
of the world rolling down my eyes

I sit alone

Why do we do this?

Poetry, like all art, is a confession that life is not enough, said a
poet from my old land, in another language
which speaks so much truth

The New Time Comes

The days are opening and my body, with my porous cells,
extends to receive the embrace of life—light shining through
the dark openings of unending winters, in this country that
sometimes becomes so cold you congeal inside and outside,
because of your being, which you maintain isolated for so long,
for fear of not understanding, or perhaps because you are a fool
looking for Utopia like the old Caballero Andante, the knight of
sad countenance who after three voyages of folly lay down and
forgot his last dream, becoming a shepherd

The new times are coming, April and then May, and I, still young
and hopeful of life and love, suddenly feel the urge to buy new
clothes and parade outside so that the knight can see me,
beautiful and begging for love, and babies too, yes, for my body is
still virgin and my blood still runs, certain every month, like the
fountain of that village I grew up in, in the highest mountains of
an old country full of rocks and a history of dictators

Clearer days, and I, enchanted by a need that comes from deep
within me scream in silence through my body and the light in my
eye, why I walk on the streets of Toronto looking for bread and
soul in the eyes of a man, intermingling with this need of mine
is the remembrance of my mother, again, you may say impatient
forgive me my mother, her veins and body exhaling years of giving
birth, eight decades of a hard life, and my father on the verge of
nonexistence, his mind giving way after years spent among the
rocks, drinking sour wine, ripe from the bellies of vines persisting
in the middle of mountains and in the fields where the sun shone
for most of the season, adorable God pressing down poor people's
pains

My body aching from a long dark winter in a country full of cold, out and in like meadows of long nights that never end, my body aching from absence, light and charcoal, long days extended under the sun of rustic skies in the other world where I came from, that land that still keeps its memory in me and I in it, like a child of the unforgetful or novels not yet written

Mays and Junes of long days, and streets clear, and I, *flâneuse* of the city, drunk on nothing, in a mediating mood strolling about, my scanty and hungry body begging for my missing love, my missing days

Beautiful I am and want to be
taken by your breath, *flâneur* of the city, lost in loneliness

Beautiful I am and want to be

Markers of Life

In the story I have not yet told you, and will never tell, because words are only shallow breaths of unenchanted messages, in that story I have dwelt in all my life, like a lost shepherdess scribbling the signs and sounds of the deep music I chant in the insides of my downward self, the place of round moons and burning suns, where trees give themselves away to me, live lovers of the lost beautiful age

In the story etched into the crevices of my fingers by Nordic winds and dry deserts, and in the earlobes seldom kissed by my lover, in that very story, in that very place, I have seen dancing in cadenced bee movements the philosophical golden stone, and the ointment vaporous form floating above my wound healing the scars of the sad stories made by the evil enchanter who made a pact with the ugly man

And in the story that I tell you here, very partially and very incompletely, I am hoping in eternal optimism that a message can pass, even if only in vagrant melancholic and sombre
shadows, that reminds you of love, of love and connection with the transcendent, that state that you and I try to find, even when we so deny, because as the poet said, poetry like all art is a confession that life is not enough

Insidious Feelings

I feel many things these days—sensations and close touches so near to my skin that I have the certainty that I am no longer alone, and all the calls I have put out, through various mediums, have finally paid off and my entire being has reached the "all is one" that the Buddhists speak of in awe and cadenced breaths of wisdoms, like the eternal deodar smells of the East Indies that have stood at the centre of the world since its very beginning, reminding us of the potency of primal love and the intensity of molecular capacity

My body and my mind inhabit one another today, a day of gains, preceded by the thousands without insight that made me feel lost and disarranged, like a vagabond dame of the eternal night, meandering through paths of the non-understanding, inhabited by nothing, a mere train moved by the cynicism of my immature self and the fever that you have displayed all this time

In this treatise that I write without a controlled order, perhaps my way of feeling today at this moment is only related to the coming of the primal season, the time of light and charcoal shadows when visions of many worlds enter each cell of my body and I, in ecstasy with the sun, dance the dance of love without the need of a man to make me reach the well that inhabits deep inside my soul, beneath the beneath of my frontal back, that place where the sorcerers of Gandhi murmur and bring sleep to their babies, who are bold and beautiful and shine out of sin in all colours of the planets, this one and the many beyond, the infinite fountain of my childhood that I went to every day countless times to bring water to the house, to myself and the many babies my mother had so we could then all stare at the sheen *resplandecente* where accumulated learning is no longer a far-fetched mirage of the anxious wizards of our time

Insidious feelings, and I lay alone and happy, certain that the spring is coming, *flâneuse* of God and the rainbows of time, *flâneuse* in perpetual *flânerie,* happy with the bucolic moment and the invisible eyes of pastors and shepherds in fields that spread vast and serene, moved by nothing, uninterrupted by the petty sorrows of the stock market, invoking the oracles of the transcendent and the reasons for life, long line of open deserts where only the wind and heat are heard and the cicadas sometimes,
when the time to mate arrives and life can no longer wait in the silence that is the belly of the world

Insidious feelings and I laugh uncontrollably – in silence, no longer waiting for you

When I Am in the Right Mood

When I am in the right mood I open my mouth and the
incantations come out in cascades of limpid water where wings of
kind angels fly me to the ether of the faraway churches of princes

When I am in the right mood I can read secrets in your words,
those you tell me in your sad days when all you can murmur
is not all you are truly feeling

In those moments the air that comes out of my dark channel is
humid and shallow like the current that guides my blood and
yours through the small veins we have all over our bodies, leaves
that know where laughter is found giving birth to the spring even
in the middle of a stubborn winter, when all seems dark and
hopeless and you miss your true home on the other side of the
Atlantic, the big ocean with ferocious and salty waves that
nothing can stop

When I am in the right mood I chant songs to you and even
though you might not be touched by them, because you dwell
in your own oblivious blank moment, I am able to know
and feel you from the bottom of my feet to the top of my soul

When I am in the right moment I know all the things that are
important and hear all the bells tolling, their sounds echoing
through the soul of my being and awakening me to the wide
vacuum, the corner where true wisdom is found

Sunny days and gargling fountains, liquid remembrances of being,
of being in the right moment

Minotaur of the Mountains

A monster of the mountains, the Minotaur visits me every time
I am unsettled and my inner line recedes into desecration, when
the tiredness of life and the routine it brings, a routine of language,
settles in and all I see is endless repetition
of death and non-sense

The corporations and the super corporations in constant debate
over territorial control and mineral hallucinations where
the shining of the rich appears and the beautiful bride of the year
strolls through the altar reaching for the blessings of the priest
and the kiss of the imperial groom

In days like these the monk on the Himalayan hills sends mute
mantras to the world through the filter of the wind in hopes that
his vision will be carried to the peoples of the planet and some
resurrection can be found at the dawn of tomorrow

My grandmother in days like these gets up from her grave which
has long lost its grass and the flowers and howls to the night
like an angry witch that just came from the nether lands to spill
venom to an already damned world

The mayor of the village, a large woman in black walking
with a cane, also gets upset at the state of affairs,
she strolls on the land yelling at her people accusing them
of not respecting the planet

Sometimes I have no choice but to cry convulsed by the grassless
graceless banks of the Tamius, let my dirt and my tiredness wash
away so I can dance again into oblivion and merge with the sky,
that open merciful azure that brings air to my lungs
and redemption to my soul

How to Walk Forward

I am at an impasse, slow and painful like nothing else I have felt
before
or so it seems because the moment is always the moment and
memory is effusive

Slow erosion of meaning and self and the confusion
of the many roads that are ahead of me, none of which seems
attractive enough to grasp and enjoy like the true lemon of life

Sinking into the dark caves of shadows where all the lines
are mixed and the executions dance like whirling unsettled snails,
dark caves of concaves, where the alphabet is Greek,
written in glyphs of other times that mean nothing to me,
leaving me stranded by the shore of Lake Mimesis—
in the labyrinth of the Bull

I can't find a memory of lighter days and brighter daisies in the
cavity of my soul
all I see are empty days and paths uncrossed or crossed that shed
no light on the mystery of my life and the life of the world

I may choose to sleep for an eternity and see if I can wake up
strong and free of the weight of planetary sorrows

Then perhaps the paths will be clean and I will feel light
like the butterfly that I am but sometimes forget

Pregnancy

My body is large with many things
thoughts and sensations, colours and full moons, remembrances
of times past when the idea of being a child was adorable
and I possessed the capacity to dwell above my limitations,
free butterfly or the pollen that serenades all our longings
when May arrives and shadows disappear to make the entire universe
ripe in full reason

My body is large, like a field of grains, ready to feed me with full
summers nourished by the caresses of my father's hands,
hands that tended them until they were ready to give life
to another, a being that would give reason to yet another,
just as when the first molecule said yes to an atom and then
to a cell ad infinitum until the multitude took over to form
a labyrinth of beings who often forget they all come from the
same fountain

My body is large and I remember secrets of past lives like the
amazing parades of the Romans and the great feasts in the Agoras
of time when Goddess Flora was adored by men ready to spill life
into the divine,
before the divine became sterile and love was forbidden by the
male God who fathered his child (or himself) transcendentally
giving Mary the light

My body is large
and the spring is coming
I open my legs and the plasma wound starts bleeding the rose-
mary of life into me, into you, making the world the best place
to live and sell roses to the hungry

The Nether Is the Nether Is not the Nether

Below my waist, deep down the curve that has no name,
or if it does, I do not know how to say it, below that very curve,
there lies the truth of wild rabbits and green frogs pulsating in the
eternal fog of long fall days, the prima dona season

My second cousin, who died when I was still a child, told me
the second coming would soon come to deliver the message that
existed long before his and mine were written and before
Christ first descended on earth

He said the second coming was always there, latent under my
skin, and if I really wanted to know it and reach the sacred
murmurs below my closed pores where the intention lies,
if I wanted that, then I should pay attention to the days that live
in complete dark nights where not even the sounds of the soft
breezes announce themselves,
pure monks in unilluminated mountains fulfilling the purest goal
of humanity

I remember my cousin telling me these words, words speaking of
non-words, un-named things trying to find the golden ring of the
ether and the nether

I used to think that he was more a child, a bigger child than me,
and foolish even if I was the one building sand castles in unstable
windy beaches and running below the circle the rain makes in
January dark days that are long, like sad widows in austere black
crying eternally by the shores of the Atlantic waiting for
nothing, because deep down they know the name and cannot
let it go and resign to the superficial euphoria of modern life or
grandiose lovers who think they know how to fight the sea but
trivialize the word Love

Love is being broken

I used to think that my cousin was a fool, a bigger fool than I who
did not know how to live in a world that had named itself using
such a narrow alphabet, forgetting the sacred murmurs under
those useless scribbles, those silent sounds that speak of the bliss
of being in nonbeing, the uncoded codes of the nether and the
ether

I used to think that . . .

But love is being broken

Speed

She wants it now, selfish that she is, oblivious to the needs
of the others and impatient with her own isolated pain

That pain that assaults us all living on this earth and fully alive
to its uncontrollable pulses

But she has been educated by the modern wizards of our time
who promise endless sunny days and the end of all pain

I try to bring reason to the season of her unreason but there is
no point, for she forever dwells in the ungraspable intrusion of
fast cars and cyborg machines, the astral media that takes away
the limits, her soul speeding her into nonexistence

I wish I could bring some sense into her, but I think I am losing
it myself, for sometimes when I am in the grip of a visceral pain,
which I ought to experience in its fullness, I resist journeying
to the source of my wound and take a jaunt to the mall and put
on the masks on sale to confuse the lost souls of our time

Speed is not what I want, not the answer to miracles that I expect,
I need help and so does she

When the World Is Tired

When the world is tired I feel its decadence upon my shoulders,
it enters me from above penetrating every fibre that is my body,
the house of my being, even when I forget, and crazed by the
fashions of the times, I implacably punish the living visceral
physicality that gives me form in this world, making me look for
bird nests and green little leaves in the zones where few enter
because of all the noises of the world

When the world is tired is it my responsibility to collect its sighs
and its screams, to anoint everyone's sores with oils from
Palestine, liquids blessed by both Allah and Jesus so that I make
all sides happy and do not speak about the quality and equality
of two Gods with two different stories, for I know that each one
is a creator and being so it chose a metaphor to evoke beauty and
the transcendence of being in its own way, but I know it is all the
same, all a matter of transcending the individual boundaries of
communication and gliding into the great well—that language of
languages

It is too much for me and I spend days crying with the falling
leaves and the naked winter trees that dance in eternal sorrow
suffering the harsh ailments of the season, I spend days crying
with the decaying life of early spring before the other life,
the new one, comes to shore, all green and eager to make a difference
in a world that has lived so long

I have dreams of people and their bodies rolling down the altar,
of blood spattered on the cross, I bathe in the blood of others
becoming but an image of profound sorrow for the world to see
and stare at, the ugly stage and the purple theatre of the forever
doomed, which no God worthy of the name can ever forget
and forgive or invent

And in other days I cannot stand my own life and I imagine my
body on the verge of dying, screaming its last screams
and breathing its last utterances, and I see how,
what in me resides that is not body or matter can go on forever,
dancing above the ether and beyond the ether, finally free
from the samsara of life

And it is that very view that saves me for the day and allows me
to continue dancing on the wheel of suffering with you,
at least we are not alone and if we live long enough and come back
enough times perhaps there is a way truly to learn from what we
do and don't do to each other, a way to finally find the final
release

The Time of the Swimming Nether

During times when I am not aware of events in my life,
I am more prone to silence your voice and enter into
the nothingness of white, round and open watermelons, where
red blood
and vigorous juice join to form the life that makes me and you
and the little ones to come

Like yesterday just before the calabash broke and my water
entered the river where I see you swimming at night, brilliant
under the full moon, always naked and unguarded because
you have attained the lightness of being, unafraid that you are
of the dejected legalists who insist on cutting the serum
that runs freely in the depths of your lower spinal cords

Or when I am in bed, between dreams and warm sheets, sliding
down to the cave of bright wells and astonishing lakes, loose
waters that bathe my entire body and soul untying the last
resistance of my selfish insecure self

Or yet at other times, when I stare at the dark sky, full of dying
stars that send me their last rays of love before entering the black
holes of existence, forever becoming the silent Madonnas of all
times, performing miracles in utter sacred darkness so that the
other world, the one where I and you live, does not lose its sight,
and we can keep strolling in gardens of incendiary greens and
breaths full of life and love and bread

It is in the nether that I swim
It is in the nether that I love the most

The Lake Within

The lake where I swim is of phosphorous pearls
I glide in them with such dexterity that I am left unforgotten
in the belly of its disappearing shine

I try to reach for my limbs and for the liquidity of my bulbous
eyes where my vision usually resides but I remain undiagnosed
through those usual methods, those learned ways I have been
using since I became an adult and forgot how to truly dance

I become blind and in that blindness I find the catharsis that I have
been missing and suddenly I see, I see with the clarity of a round
light bulb or the fullness of a moon in its ripe season

I reach out to nothing and I cry to the wolves whose stare I have
dreamed over and over again during nights that have passed by
me, nights where alone I was able to enter the channel that has no
end and no beginning and which allows me to dance with the
saints

The Clarity of Language

When alone and utterly concentrated on the world and its true
meaning, I enter a zone of luminosity and salvation

A terrain of novel ideas and I learn how to attain the levity of
the angels, my body floating above and my mind coming to
encounter the universe and suddenly I forget who I am only to
remember more exactly where I came from and who are my true
brothers and my true sisters

I dance and swim in midair among the pollen and the lost
butterflies, and in a moment only I attain the sanctity of Sor Juana
Inés de la Cruz or the burning fluorescent halo of Joan of Arc

I become Nostradamus and see the future and the past of the
universe, all its history in my being cell by cell making me
a kindly witch who carries in her all that is, all that was, all that
will be

I am one person, one continent, one world, one sea, one galaxy,
one universe
No longer do I cry or yearn for the missing missed link, because in
one sole instant I become the pregnant bride of the one sole God

I fly and I dance and I roll on the floor, because all air, all matter,
and all movement know no boundaries and all that there is is all
that I am, all that I can enter

There is nothing left to be or to attain
All is complete

I have restored the Great Pangaea

Incandescent Crying

Come to me when I am alone in the midst of unending fog and
dark clouds
I have called you several times, ready to love and pour life into the
world
I have written lines of unfulfilled poems and danced naked in the
rain calling your shadow to me and caressing your unending body
with solemn fingers that work feathery magic

Come to me when I am ready like I was, when
I was ready and alone and I opened myself to you eager for
a glimpse of white teeth and open laughter, after years of utter
isolation and crying solitude

Like a fool I became entrenched in your word game and the
promises of your confusion, like a child eager for the smell
of moist fresh spring when the air brings news of other beautiful
worlds and far away possibilities, I crave beauty like poems
of unending words that no one has yet written

I stared at you with clean eyes and hands ready to touch the
limpid marrow of love, that translucent liquid that is the giver of
life, I danced in the waters of my own imaginary, incendiary love
affair and I took what you said like pearls from a man ready to try
what the world offers him in a gold platter like mines of ancient
galleries with Mayan gods performing miracles of magic,
bringing cooper to the starving and messages from the Sun God

I read roses of clean alphabets in your marked fingers and shining
eyes, perfect amulets to my needy philosophical stone, like a fool
or a child, eager to touch truth and be touched with clean real
hands, manipulating me into the oblivion of centuries where love
affairs have permeated the solitary lines of interminable times

How can I live in this world that fools me every time I open myself like a rose smelling clean cherries, wanting to enter the wide Garden of Eve?

How can I bathe myself in God's incense when pain bites my deepest soul every time?

Today in the midst of profound pain and mourning the love that again failed me, I enter the embrace of solitude, perhaps forever I cry for you, a cry as deep as the well of life and sorrow, that life and sorrow that Isabel Allende, the priestess of melancholia, sings so well about in her treatments of the human condition

I cry for you, imagine you will come and get me and bathe me with kisses and incendiary greens

I will heal again because life is beautiful, and so am I
as my grandmother would remind me

My grandmother, who died having lived a long life alone and raised two daughters on her own—the same line that I belong to, because I am the sister of Nívea and Clara, Blanca and Alba, and Rosa the Beautiful, women who forever live in the unending chanting poetry of their mistress, because words can perform miracles

I will heal again because the world is round and in its unending wheel I will finally find my true kind King, and become the Queen of times—when love will be stronger than hate and understanding stronger than misunderstanding

I will heal again—and I will dance in the circular trail of those who have found the truth and the secret to being loved by the master of the universe

The Bearable Lightness of Being

There is a light within me
It is pure and beautiful and has guided me through the hardest
times of my life
It has told me how strong and beautiful I am, it has showed me
how the sun sends light to my sad eyes to illuminate the world I
live in

There is a light within me, of cadent particles, rainbows that
descend upon me so I don't die when harsh shadows infiltrate
my walking line and break the soul of my skin, leaving raw veins
open to the knife cuts the world inflicts upon the sanctity of my
body

Sometimes it feels as though the light is leaving me:
I lie naked, crawling on the floor calling on love and God for
reason and incantation, I feel nausea enter every pore of my being
and my body wants to throw up the sad stories you gave me and
the confusion your mind transposed to mine like the others ones
did, making me so insecure that the light within me barely flickers
and my ancestral plane, the one that takes me far away to shinning
galaxies and endless rivers, almost stops, and I am a prisoner of
low terrains and sullied souls

I lie there, a forlorn creature who has lost her way
I send faint messages to Maria, the Mother of God, hoping she
will descend upon me and wipe my tears and my body, make it
clean again for the next blow of life and sorrow, as she did with
her beloved son

I call the sages of old Africa through the sacred murmurs of lost
beautiful languages that I am able to resuscitate from the corners

of my being, because I come from that continent and I still remember even though I have been wandering since my birth a sorrowful nomad, a vagabond who has forever lost her way and forgotten her own navel

I send messages to my father who died only after he had shown me how much he truly loved me, I could see that love in his eyes, those open staring and glittering eyes that people have when they are near death and can see the fogginess of the other side and the clarity of life in this small corner of the universe, this place where we keep bleeding like endless open veins that know nothing but
sorrow

I do this and that, and much more, I do all I can think and dream of to ward off bad memories and empty words of confused lovers promising what they do not have in themselves to give

I lie there an eternity, soaked in hurt, blood and bad memories invoking the things that truly give me life and being, and then very slowly I see my light emerging, first like a timid bride barely showing the laces of her white dress, and then gradually revealing all the pureness and whiteness that live within me, making me fully alive, ready to dance again, and love

This is what makes my life bearable
This is the bearable lightness of my being
I must sing a song
to thank God again

Time

Time comes and goes and I sit here undulating under its
unforgiving waves
I watch the landscape and the goats that roam in the green
pastures because it's still early and the grass still lives, for them and
for me

I caress the fog and the air of the harsh mountainous wind,
hoping to catch, if only for a moment, the life that evades us all
from morning to dawn, like a beautiful fragrance that cannot last
forever and which when caught ceases to be

Time comes and goes like the blank floor on which I write its
passage, leaving it filled with memories of what it is, or what it
appears to be at that precise moment, until one day centuries of
lunar movements erase its messages, leaving it white again,
waiting for the impurities of your life to be inscribed in a pure
canvas

"To wait for God, the mind must become naked," as someone
once said in a moment of revelation

The Walls of Nothing

I live in a house that is old: I smell the breaths of old lost souls
meandering on the walls of ancient granite, built by the Romans,
or others who came before or after them, attempting to tame the
earth

I shiver with cold and anticipation of my days when I enter the
realm of nonphysical existence and all I have is the ephemeral
lightness of being, scarce candles piercing through the winter days

I roam around the house trying to catch the zones not yet
inhabited by those marks that have left and now cling to life on
the walls of nothing as if observing life idly and laughing at how
cruel it can be

I caress the walls to feel the slightness of my evading being yearning
for my time to come so that I too can laugh at all of us, mere
mortals who suffer constantly under the pressure of heavy blood
and throbbing vessels

I call out to you, my invisible saints, living in the paths of nothingness
so that you can call me soon to your realm, where nothing weighs
and where horses, white and black, run in synchrony, beautiful
dancers of the forever nether

The Day of the Death

The days of a red blasting sun were those that she preferred

The intensity of the burning fire reminded her of Dante's Inferno,
when he described the divine comedy of being human

She looked above with her eyes wide open, praying for God
to deliver her from suffering

Life under the clouds had been tiresome for her soul and she did
not have energy left to continue walking the stony roads of the
place she had been forced to dwell in when her mother opened
her legs and delivered her on the dirty wooden floor

The floor of that old house, soiled with other births before hers
of boys and girls who would live a long life
feeling the pains of all
because they came to this world under the reign of the Fascist

Nothing Surpasses Nothingness

In that state of blank stare I sing songs of lilac peace: white and
clean songs that tell me of the beautiful thereafter:
after the clouds, after the sun, after the stars

In that space between the lines I gargle with fresh water in my
throat and revise my central thesis in distraction

On the train to the great city of ancient Rome I find kings and
queens that salute my innocence and place red carpets before
my naked feet to protect my sensitive soles from the dust of the
streets

On my dream to the Nether Lands I encounter a lost white
flower, tiny and yet fundamentally necessary, the first one to
appear on earth, which then taught the birds how to make the
planet truly beautiful

During the full season of yellow genistas, when white and yellow
romarias cover the vast land, I converse with my hungry goats
about the delicacies of the world: they listen, with eyes and ears,
chewing the flowers

And during the dark winters, I pray in silent obscurity with
curtains drawn so I may find the tiny filter of light in the most
unprocured places of my wide, wide home

Philosopher's Sculptures

The religious philosophers do not know enough atheism to find in it the fundamental spirituality of life

They meander through lines of sacred books, from the Book of Leviticus to the other Bible, from the Quran to the Shield of Mammy Water, and still they remain incapable of arriving at this most divine conclusion: that nothing is essentially divine and everything is relationally godly

The new ones, throwing stones at the police and carving holes on their bodies, ambulatory graffiti denouncing the traumas of capitalism, scream obscenities to the lords of this world, but in vain, because as Nietzsche said, God is indeed dead

Sometimes I too want to forget my blood running through the lines, and enter the zone of no return, the zone of nonbelief, and then finally laugh uncontrollably at the destiny of men and women

Whistling Through the Fields

I walk steadily through the fields of my infancy trying to
recapture the sounds and colours of bygone games

I walk through the green cornfields trying to remember the
dreams I dreamed or the novels I wrote using metaphors never
seen, stunningly beautiful, and yet no one ever gave them due
respect or chanted them in church along with the equally sublime
sermons of Padre Lévito, which I would listen to with eager eyes
and elevated feet, a girl in awe of magic

I whistle to myself the lines of the land I walked on when I was
eager to learn everything the world could teach, because
everything was beautiful

I whistle myself through this guided melancholia

In this moment of the blank present, I whistle, try to find
metaphors for the poem that I truly need, the wind that I truly
crave

And perhaps through the breath in my nose and the air of my
mouth, the perfect poem will be born and my novel will see the
light of day

It will live, as it lived when I was the child of an invisible God,
attentively listening to Padre Lévito with eager eyes and raised feet,
a girl in awe of magic

A Word for You (at the End of the Year)

She may not always say what she means
and yet she means to say well
to say without voices imposing
without the chain of language that cuts through our thoughts
and shows our true ways of being

To say without fear, speak from the bottom of a complex and full
well
where life and feeling cannot be measured so neatly, so completely

In her (sometimes) confused and (almost) always multifaceted
way of being
and in her profound desire to connect deeply with YOU, others
and otherness
she will say things openly, speak freely from a mind that wants to
remain untamed and run free

Pure molecular brain cells telling and speaking, searching and
remembering memories of times transcendent through a twisted
uttering tongue

Or unframed visions like water in a formless sea where the clean
serum makes life a fountain of whirling renewal

But she means no disrespect and no harm
she only means things, multiple things
unformed, un-finalized currents of thoughts, reminiscences,
casualties of life
she wants to explore, to understand and to question
life, moments, people, ideas, feelings

And in that need to babble about everything and everyone
she may get and sound confused and annoying
and she may unwittingly hurt those she values the most

Days of Loss

Throughout the year there are days of loss
days of loss and meditation when you stop feeling high
and suddenly collapse, do not want to get up to see the world,
tired of seeing face after face running from here to there and back

You are tired of the same smells, the same streets, the same dead
gardens where the hydrangeas have long forgotten how to bloom
in astonishing colours that make you forget where you are and
even why your mother calls your name

What you want in these days is to stay in darkness, shaded from
all that screams and all the shit that interrupts the peace of your
white venous flow, those cloudy states that may very well be the
definition of heaven on earth

What you want is to shield the untouched part of your being
from the degradation of the fast life, a walk that never stops,
never stares, never incubates its own eggs to discover how giving
birth to new lambs can be fundamentally necessary, making the
spring not a season to be dismissed by the hurry of the world

There are days of loss and darkness so intrinsic to being that to
miss them is to miss love all together and die without ever having
slowed down to hear the silence that lies in the dark caves of
concave untamed flows, where you find meaning in nothingness
and touch the pulsating visionary cadent particles that lift you
above the ground

There are days of loss and light just like this which you cannot af-
ford to miss because if you do you may very well have just passed
by without ever having smelled the small white roses whose

colour can only be discerned in the darkest corners of being
Secret that only the wise can find

Watermarks

I take water into my soul
and I watch it like marbles full of lines between which I live
I bathe in the severity of that liquid of ancient memories
lives that have run to me, to this moment, to this line,
so that I can hear in the vibrations of the world the tenderness
and disdain of people

All those who came from the long line steadily to me so
my loneliness would be appeased and I and you could join in
together
and write the novel of life

From beginning to end, from end to beginning, before the nothing
and at the peak of intense throbbing and after the big oceanic
break, the universal earthquake, when many forces clashed,
in a moment of unseen molecular love,
to give birth to infinity

A circle, a cycle of serene seas
or thunderous announcements
a rose of life
a novel of many novels

The Cracking of the Earth

The craters are falling apart
I see them crumbling down and I am afraid of the doom to come

I see long lines of people entering the nothingness where we all
came from
I nestle among the trees, trying to prolong the life of my isolated
self,
to hold on to some solitary dignity

My feet touch the humid ground where fresh moss still grows
I allow my naked soles to marvel at the sounds that come from
the earth's core
I feel the muddy fiery energy in its primeval state before plants
even existed and all was liquid matter quivering with the elements
of the fundamental table

I lie down on a vertical line listening to the silences of the others
I feel less alone now, less crushed, less myself

Tomorrow the day will break and I, a wanderer on this planet,
will stare at the skies to hear murmurs of the gods

I will die then, perfectly happy that I have lived
and walked the earth
with the ants

It Is Spring

It is spring and I want to give blood
life pouring out of me to pay back the earth for the beautiful
season
to feed the children dying under the boots of dictators
girls and boys who still believe that life is forever a clear ring
season
where dancing is all
to feed the thin birds emerged from the dark hunger of long
winter
to water the plants bursting out of the moist soil

It is spring and I want to give blood
a saint offering her body, making your thirst invisible to the sins of
your past days

It is spring and I want to dance with my feet in the mud
my arm opening itself to the cleansing shower of the New Year
abundant benevolent rain loving me
cell by cell and I enchanted by its moist musical cadence
cascading upon me, magnificent reminders of long gone sages
who knew nothing but love and its transcendental secrets and life
upon life upon life

I want to chant in silence paying homage to the forces that make
everything happen
and never forget to visit when the days get darker, when it seems
impossible to continue and all I want is to remain in bed hiding under
the dark sheets of non-life like a dead cat

I want to go to bed late and wake up early to smell the geraniums
under my window

and look carefully and slowly at the breeze that walks in the
morning and evening dusk
when darkness and brightness are married and mystery tells me in
roundabout ways that there is a lot in this world—I become
the Dulcinea, beautiful, proud, and a believer

I want to go to bed late and get up early and have long days and
nights
to lay down on the earth and hear the secrets of life moving in
prefect rhythms to the surface to greet you and me,
the poor orphans of the seasons

It is spring and all I want to do is give blood
the most precious substance I can offer
the red crimson under my beautiful skin

It is spring and suddenly all I want to do is give blood
to you

The Curious Book

There is a book on the shelf that is unlike the others
I can tell by the spine that is wearing out its wings, as though the book itself contains not enough knowledge and is reaching out to others to peek at their lines in an attempt to decipher the mysteries of the world, which are many, ancient and so profound

The other books, as though jealous of the God they know, like mean-spirited insecure priests, do not freely open themselves to this curious thing, but hold themselves tightly together, become closer to neighbours on the same shelf,
those not so eager to reach the bottomless pit that is our universe

I sit on my old sofa, which is also wretched in its own condition, and I watch this spectacle in silence, savouring the ways of the curious book and the manner in which its brothers and sisters
lie in their sleep, satisfied with their self-contained knowledge, like premature dead children or perhaps cynical elders who have learned that curiosity can kill

And it is in this reminiscing that I remember my father Adelino, recall how happy he was, just knowing his cows, using their dung to seal off the oven in which we baked corn bread that exhaled the sublime scent of the mountains where the cows had gone grazing only the day before

I recall his shiny eyes and how he said that happiness and good living can be found in the most unlikely places and fools are those who keep going in circles and circles trying to unveil what must remain closed from the eye of reason, primal dogs who cannot stop trying to catch their own tails even when they grow old

You Call Me at Night

You call me at night through veins of memories
clusters of cherries pouring down upon my body, candles kissing the border of my soul
a blanket of clean water washing down my solitude
I become full, filled with you and them, through the summers of my life

Veins upon veins upon veins in a long line of the sweet wine that we made all our lives
so that men and women, brothers and sisters, mothers and fathers
would not die of thirst in lonely homes

You call me at night through porous cells that become fingers and toes, blue and brown eyes, translucent stories that tell all the hardships that the body and the soul have had to endure, washing sorrows and watching life go by, hard as it was during those days of rocky mountains and fascist dictators sending the boys, brother Z and brother A, down there to Africa to defend a land that was never theirs

You call me at night through veins of memories, you throw them around like pulsating witnesses to an unforgettable life that gives and gives and gives again, blood, water and plasma in one single blanket of Yes

You call me at night like a marvel of the underground, sprinkling life upon death, and yes-es upon no-es

You call me at night with love for memory, your body showing in twists and shadows, your eyes pouring remembrances upon my closed sleepy eyes, filling my house with laughing children and ancestral stories of coal made by hand and dirty miners buried underneath their need for bread and water, beautiful lives that only music can tell

You call me at night when I roll the rosary desperately around my hands invoking prayers to Isabel and imagining the hydrangeas that were put upon her black thick hair when she was buried prematurely under the mud that then ate up what was left of her long suffering body, whose grave and fatal illnesses no doctor could diagnose, because the greatest secrets belong only to God

I speak Hail Marys and Our Fathers, dozens of them, like long lines of meadows of clean hay, without you there is nothing, only intemporal silence feeding an unbearable nothingness

It's with love that I receive you meandering through my bed making me a sensual liquid being, roses upon roses, upon roses, the hydrangeas of Isabel falling on me, and I a bride of the Levant where the sun comes from and Scheherazade was a Virgin full of the lust for life and poetry to tell

You call me at night and I hear you

The Quilt

This quilt
is endowed with powers that will shake the faith of the atheists
powers that can break your silences
and bring you the bibles of times past
when Jesus lived on earth
and Mohamed delivered his sacred news

This quilt sings my present
with the songs of the past
the dark colours of winters gone
when rains played with my girlish ears
and gave me the messages of the messengers

This quilt adorns my present
with dresses I wore in past springs

Some were made by my great-aunt Camila
with laces and measured measures
always hugging my different bodies
each spring as I became aware of the boys
their smells and their searching eyes
their greedy hands
that too wanted to
dress my body

This quilt was made by my grandmother
the one with blue eyes
who in her constant search for new lines
always used the old weaver's loom
to produce scandalous life
from old clothes

The Unkind God

She gets up every morning
fresh out of her dream world
and runs to the altar to worship her unkind god

She spends precious minutes birthing
this god whom she adores, who speaks to her in a language no
one can understand but her

And every morning when she leaves the altar she is sad
she has missed the birthing of the day

They ask, why does she adore this rude ruler?
Why does she sing the prayers that make her cry?
Why doesn't she run away?
They say

But they can't hear the god's message
they don't know this god is not like the others
this god is made of iron
this being is deadly
punishing her with long prayers

Until he drinks away her waters
until he satiates his profane hunger
until he feels he can blow her away with a simple breath
and every morning she gets up early to adore him
and she misses the birth of the sun
and she forgets to speak to the lilies
and to milk the cows
and to laugh with the stars
dance with the goats
salute the moon

drink papayas
eat the sea

At night when she comes back home she is exhausted
having spent the day sweating and running away
fighting the machines inside a narrow dark room
full of mirrors *fantasmagóricos*
and doctors in white with cold fingers
so much iron,
melting it cutting it wasting it away like that
and the next morning it will begin again
just before the sun starts searching for the softness of her curves
with research so careful, eyes so gentle

So rude this ruler . . . so unkind this god

Irene Marques holds a PhD in Comparative Literature, a Masters in French Literature, a Masters in Comparative Literature and a Bachelor of Social Work. She is a bilingual writer (English and Portuguese) and has taught African and Caribbean literatures, comparative and world literature, literary theory, and writing and rhetoric at the Ontario College of Art and Design University for the past seven years. Her academic publications include the edited volume *The Works of Chin Ce: A Critical Overview* (2007), the manuscript *Transnational Discourses on Class, Gender, and Cultural Identity* (2012) and numerous articles in international journals including *African Identities: Journal of Economics, Culture and Society, Research in African Literatures,* and *CLCWeb: Comparative Literature and Culture.* Her published works of fiction include *Wearing Glasses of Water* (poetry, 2007), *Habitando na Metáfora do Tempo: Crónicas Desejadas* (short stories, 2009) and *The Circular Incantation* (prose poetry, 2013).